Shakespeare's
A Midsummer Night's Dream
A Prose Narrative

by Peter V.T. Kahle

Illustrated by Barbara Nickerson

Seventy Fourth Street Productions

Seattle, Washington

Books by Seventy Fourth Street Productions
are available directly from the Publisher:

Seventy Fourth Street Productions LLC

350 North 74th Street
Seattle, Washington 98103

206-781-1447 *phone/fax*

Design and production:

Deb Figen, ART & DESIGN SERVICE
Seattle, Washington

Publisher's Cataloging-in-Publication Data

Kahle, Peter V. T.
    Shakespeare's A midsummer night's dream : a prose narrative / by
Peter V.T. Kahle ; illustrated by Barbara Nickerson.
    p. cm.
    ISBN 0-9655702-0-7

    1. Shakespeare, William, 1564-1616--Adaptations.   I. Title.
II. Title: Midsummer night's dream : a prose narrative

PR2878.M54K34 1997   813,'54
                        QBI96-40771

ISBN 0-9655702-0-7

FIRST EDITION
Printed in the United States of America
01 00 99 98 97   5 4 3 2 1

Acknowledgment

SEVENTY FOURTH STREET PRODUCTIONS
would like to acknowledge Joseph and Hilda Kahle,
who helped us make this dream come true.
In them lives the spirit of the late Angus Bowmer,
founder of the Oregon Shakespeare Festival.
When asked if he ever dreamed that
the two plays he put on in Ashland in 1932
would grow into such a great festival,
Angus replied, "My dreams are open-ended."

Introduction

A Midsummer Night's Dream is the ideal play with which to introduce a child to Shakespeare. It is the most beloved and the most frequently performed of all of Shakespeare's plays. It contains the great comic characters Puck and Nick Bottom, magic and fairies, getting lost in the wood, and above all, the marvelous words. This is the door into a world of wonders.

Shakespeare represents the pinnacle of human achievement — and his works, these timeless stories, are our legacy as creatures of passion and imagination. We celebrate the power and beauty in Shakespeare, and are thrilled to share projects like this book with his young fans at our performances. Here's to their playful and joyful retelling!

Terry Edward Moore and Paul T. Mitri
Co-Artistic Directors
SEATTLE SHAKESPEARE FESTIVAL

FOREWORD

To Parents

If you love theatre, you know that taking children to see a play is giving them a gift that will last all their lives. The experience of live theatre, with actors and lights, costumes and scenery, and most of all the words, the spoken words, can light the flame of a child's imagination. And if you love theatre and beautiful words, one gift you want to give a child is *A Midsummer Night's Dream*. It's a love story and a comedy with some of Shakespeare's most lyric lines and some of his funniest, too, phrases he coined that became part of our language forever.

To aid children in making the most of seeing the play and hearing the wonderful language, it would help if they knew the story. This book is *A Midsummer Night's Dream* retold as a story, so a child can follow the tangled web of lovers and fairies and working men. It includes as many favorite lines as possible, so the sound and flavor of the dialogue will be familiar when the child sees the actual play.*

To help yourself and your child enjoy this book, read it out loud, first, to yourself. That way, you'll know the story and can do a good dramatic reading. Have fun with it. Make up different voices for some of the characters, particularly ones you like. Let the speech fall trippingly off your tongue — it will, you know.

If you want to put on a scene of your own after you've finished the book, look in the EPILOGUE after the play and at the PLAY SCRIPTS in the envelope in the back of the book.

---

* NOTE: The dialogue in quotes is based upon Howard Staunton's edition (November 1857-May 1860). It has been abridged and amended to fit the short narrative form.

Shakespearean theatres were outdoors.

They had no roofs and no electric lights.

PROLOGUE

This is a story about dreams. When you say the word "dream," you might mean some thoughts or pictures that came to your mind while you were sleeping. You know how strange, how funny or scary they can be. But to me the word "dream" might mean my fondest hope, that is, I dream of marrying my special sweetheart or I dream of becoming an actor. This is a story about both kinds of dreams. This is a story of Kings and Queens, Dukes and common folk, fairies and mortals, and lovers and angry fathers, who all got mixed up with magic on a warm, soft midsummer night in the forest.

Have you ever gone to the theatre to see a play, a story acted out right in front of your eyes? People come from near and far, all dressed up for a special occasion. The members of the audience file in and take their seats, and the murmur of anticipation rises louder and louder. Those who have coughs put cough drops in their mouths and keep extras in their pockets, so they won't disturb the play.

Some of the best plays in the world were written by a man named William Shakespeare. He lived more than four hundred years ago, but he wrote such great plays that people still love them and go to see them. One of his best-loved plays is called *A Midsummer Night's Dream*. This book is William Shakespeare's play, told as a story.

Some of the words may sound strange. Four hundred years ago, people said "thee" instead of "you," or "thy" instead of "your." A big donkey was called an "ass," and so was a stupid man. A "joiner" was a workman who made doors and windows, things that needed to be joined snugly together.

Because Shakespeare was a poet, he wrote his plays in verses and rhymes and he used unusual words because of their beautiful sounds. They come clear as you listen to them or if you say them aloud to yourself. Thyself. See? These are words that need to be spoken out loud.

Some of the characters' names are strange, too, if you look at them on the CAST OF CHARACTERS page. They are long-ago names used to make these characters seem long-ago in time, even for Shakespeare's day. You could sound them out yourself, or look at page 69 for the PRONUN-CIATION GUIDE to see how to pronounce them.

Theatres have changed a great deal since *A Midsummer Night's Dream* was first performed. Theatres then were outdoors with no roofs. There were no electric lights. Plays had to be put on during the day, so you had to pretend about night. Men played all the parts, even the women's parts, so you had to pretend about that, too.

In our modern theatre, people rustle through their programs to find out who the characters are, and the names of the actors and actresses who will portray them. The actors and actresses have practiced and rehearsed. They must memorize every word they will say, every step, or turn, or look they will make. The characters all work together to act out the story. If you'd like to see what the actors would use to learn their parts, look in the envelope inside the back cover for the PLAY SCRIPTS.

A play is a chance for everyone in the audience to pretend. You know you haven't suddenly gone back 2000 years to the ancient city of Athens. You are sitting in the theatre. But if you're willing to pretend, then the actors can use that pretending to make a kind of magic. They can create a whole world and invite you into it.

All at once the lights go dim, all the way to dark, and everyone gets quiet. Then the lights come up, the curtain opens, and the magic begins. And the best part is that the audience is part of making the magic, right along with the actors.

Cast of Characters in the Play

Dramatis Personae

THESEUS, *Duke of Athens*
HIPPOLYTA, *Queen of the Amazons, betrothed to Theseus*
EGEUS, *father of Hermia*

LYSANDER, *in love with Hermia*
DEMETRIUS, *in love with Hermia, favored by her father, Egeus*
HERMIA, *in love with Lysander*
HELENA, *in love with Demetrius*
OBERON, *King of the Fairies*
TITANIA, *Queen of the Fairies*
PUCK, *or* ROBIN GOODFELLOW, *a most mischievous sprite*

PEASEBLOSSOM	*Four*
COBWEB	*fairies*
MOTH	*attending*
MUSTARDSEED	*Titania*

PETER QUINCE, *a carpenter*	
NICK BOTTOM, *a weaver*	*as PYRAMUS*
FRANCIS FLUTE, *a bellows-mender*	*as THISBY*
TOM SNOUT, *a tinker*	*as WALL*
SNUG, *a joiner*	*as LION*
ROBIN STARVELING, *a tailor*	*as MOONSHINE*

Scene

The city of Athens and the Palace Wood nearby.

The old man's name was Egeus,
and he came before the Duke with a grave complaint
against his daughter, Hermia.

ACT I

Scene 1

ONG AGO THERE LIVED A GREAT and noble man, the good Duke Theseus, who ruled the ancient city of Athens. Duke Theseus had defeated the fierce Amazon women in battle and taken prisoner their Queen, Hippolyta. Being as wise and compassionate as he was bold and brave, and being moved by her strength and beauty, Theseus fell in love with Hippolyta and she returned that love. They were to marry in four days, with the coming of the new moon.

Duke Theseus and Queen Hippolyta sat in the great hall of his palace. Even there they could hear the noise of celebration from the streets. All Athens was dancing and singing and playing to honor the approaching wedding. Everyone in the city prepared some poem or rehearsed a play in hopes of being chosen to entertain the happy royal couple. Every face was smiling, or so it seemed.

Just then, an angry old man entered, tugging a petite dark-haired girl by her arm. The old man's name was Egeus, and he came before the Duke with a grave complaint against his daughter, Hermia. He had promised Hermia's hand in marriage to Demetrius, a rich, handsome young man of the city. But she refused to marry him. She had fallen in love with another man, Lysander.

Old Egeus called forth the two young men, blond Demetrius and dark Lysander, who glared at each other.

Egeus demanded that he be granted the power of the ancient law of Athens: if Hermia refused to obey her father and would not marry Demetrius, she must die.

Theseus said, "What say you, Hermia? Demetrius is a worthy gentleman."

"So is Lysander," replied Hermia.

"In himself he is," said Theseus, "but without your father's consent, the other must be held the worthier."

Said Hermia, "I would my father looked but with my eyes."

Theseus could see that Hermia loved Lysander, but the law was the law. If she refused to marry Demetrius, Hermia must die or else enter a nunnery and never marry any man. This he told her.

Hermia grew pale, but she stood very straight. "My soul consents not," she said.

"Relent, sweet Hermia," cried Demetrius. "Lysander, yield to my right."

Lysander's dark eyes flashed angrily. "You have her father's love, Demetrius," he said. "Let me have Hermia's. You marry him."

Lysander appealed to the Duke, and his case was strong. He was as rich as Demetrius. His family was just as good, and more than that, Hermia loved him. And besides, Demetrius was once in love with Hermia's best friend, Helena. Demetrius had won her heart and soul. Helena loved him still, though he had turned away from her.

Demetrius looked embarrassed, but he said nothing. Theseus stood up and gathered his robes around him. He gave Hermia just four days to decide what she would do.

"Fit your fancies to your father's will," said Theseus, "or else the law of Athens yields you up to death or to a vow of single life."

The Duke offered his arm to Queen Hippolyta and called Demetrius and Egeus to come consult with him. The rest of the court followed, leaving Hermia and Lysander alone.

Hermia almost wept, for the choice she faced was bitterly cruel. Lysander tried to comfort her.

"The course of true love never did run smooth," he told her, and speaking sweet words he showed her that the troubles they faced only proved that they were lovers true. But more than mere comfort, Lysander had a plan.

"I have a widowed aunt," he said. "From Athens is her house remote seven leagues. There, gentle Hermia, may I marry thee; and to that place the sharp Athenian law cannot pursue us. Steal forth from thy father's house tomorrow night, and in the forest will I wait for thee."

And Hermia answered, "Good Lysander, I swear to thee by Cupid's strongest bow, tomorrow truly will I meet with thee."

Yet as they made their plans, Helena came upon them. She was Hermia's best friend all through school, though tall, blond Helena was as unlike short, dark Hermia as two girls could be. Helena was miserable, for she loved Demetrius with all her heart, and yet he would not look at her.

"The more I love, the more he hates me," she lamented.

"Take comfort," said Hermia. "He no more shall see my face: Lysander and myself will fly this place." And she told Helena all their plans.

But when she was alone again, Helena was made so foolish by her love, she thought, I will tell Demetrius and win his thanks, and so turn his attention back to me. She little dreamed what twists and turns magic and a midsummer night had in store.

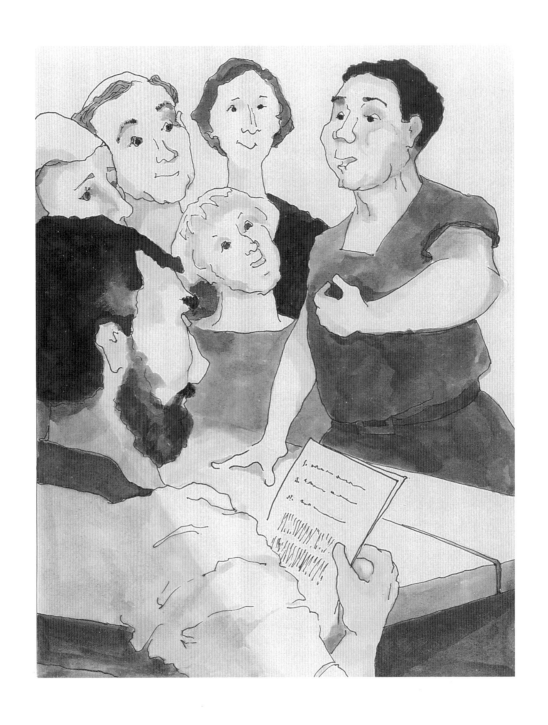

Bottom leaped up again.

"Let me play the lion too."

ACT I

Scene 2

THAT SAME DAY six men of Athens met in the cottage of Peter Quince, a carpenter. They were rough, hard-working men in homespun clothes, more suited to lift and carry than to act out a love story. But they were determined to do what they could to entertain their Duke, as they said, "on his wedding day at night." The men who met in the cottage of Peter Quince were Francis Flute, the bellows-mender; Robin Starveling, the tailor; Tom Snout, the tinker, and a joiner named Snug. The last to arrive, though the most important in all their eyes — including his own — was Nick Bottom, the weaver.

"Our play," Peter Quince told the others, "is 'The most lamentable comedy, and most cruel death of Pyramus and Thisby.'"

"A very good piece of work I do assure you, and a merry one," said Nick Bottom. Lamentable means sad, and what a sad comedy might be, or how a cruel death could be merry, he did not explain. "Call forth your actors," he said.

Peter Quince said, "You, Nick Bottom, are set down for Pyramus, a lover that kills himself most gallant for love."

It was the most important part, and all the others were convinced that no man in Athens but Bottom could play it.

"Let the audience look to their eyes: I will move storms!" cried Bottom. He told them he would rather play a tyrant, and he leaped up and bellowed some fierce words to show how he would have done it. But there were no tyrants in their play, so he would be the lover.

Francis Flute was told he must play Thisby, the lady that Pyramus must love. Francis Flute was the youngest and fairest of face of them all, but he did not look like a lady. Quince told him he might wear a mask and speak in a high little voice.

Bottom leaped up. "If I may hide my face, let me play Thisby too: I'll speak in a monstrous little voice." He spoke on in high, squeaky tones, "'Ah, Pyramus, my lover dear, thy Thisby dear, and lady dear.'"

"No, no," said Quince, "you must play Pyramus, and you, Flute, Thisby."

As all the others agreed, Bottom was forced to sit down. He sat still, but he muttered to himself, as Robin Starveling was cast to play Thisby's mother and Tom Snout, Pyramus' father. Last of all, Snug, the joiner, was told he would play the part of the lion. They must learn their parts by tomorrow night, Quince told them, so they could rehearse their play.

"Have you the lion's part written?" asked Snug, anxiously. "Pray you, if it be, give it me: for I am slow of study."

"It is nothing but roaring," replied Peter Quince.

Bottom leaped up again. "Let me play the lion too. I will roar so that I will make the Duke say, 'Let him roar again: let him roar again!'"

Peter Quince said quickly, "If you fright the duchess and the ladies, they would shriek: and that were enough to hang us, every mother's son."

"But I will aggravate my voice," said Bottom. The more excited he got, the more he used long words, not always the right ones. "I will aggravate my voice so, that I will roar as gently as any sucking dove. I will roar as 'twere a nightingale."

Peter Quince sighed. "You can play no part but Pyramus," he said. Then he reminded them all they must keep their plans a secret from the rest of the town and they must all learn their parts. "Con them by tomorrow night," he said, "and meet me in the palace wood, a mile beyond the town, by moonlight; there we will rehearse."

"We will meet," Bottom proclaimed grandly, "and there we may rehearse obscenely and courageously. Take pains, be perfect: adieu."

ACT II

Scene 1

THE PALACE WOOD was a small forest just beyond the palace gates. Duke Theseus loved to hunt there with his hounds. His court and the people of the city loved to walk in the shade of the green leaves. It was a place for young people to meet, accidentally on purpose, or for a man to quarrel with his brother, without half the town knowing all their business. That was why the young lovers, Hermia and Lysander, chose to meet there, to escape from Athens. That was why jealous Demetrius chased after them there, and forsaken Helena after him. That was why the cast of the play, Peter Quince and Bottom and the others, went to rehearse there. None of them realized that the palace wood was a different place at night.

The forest by day was cool and pleasant, where paths wound through groves of tall trees, with here and there a clearing full of grass and wildflowers, and over everything a golden green light. The forest by night was dark and mysterious, where paths wound in circles to nowhere, toadstools glowed of their own light, and dewdrops on a spider web gleamed like pearls in the pale rays of the moon. Duke Theseus was a mortal man, and he owned the forest by day; but Oberon, King of the Fairies, ruled the night.

Oberon was wise and powerful, with great knowledge of spells and magic and ancient lore. He had many servants, fairies, sprites, hobgoblins and other People of the Hills at his command. Chief among them was a prankish spirit called Robin Goodfellow, also known as Puck.

Though he was wise, Oberon was as prone to jealousy and anger as any foolish man. All spring the land had suffered his wrath, for he was angry at Titania, Queen of the Fairies. One of Titania's ladies had given birth to a son by an Indian king. The child lived, but the lady died. Oberon wanted the boy to become his knight and trace the forests wild with him, but Titania refused. She kept the child close beside her, made him all her joy, and shut Oberon out.

Therefore, Oberon had lashed the land with rain until the rivers overflowed in floods and the green corn rotted in the fields. Only now had he finally allowed the warm, blossom-scented summer to appear. King Oberon and Queen Titania had come together from the ends of the earth to bless the wedding of Theseus and Hippolyta, but they never met in grove or green without such fierce argument that all the elves crept into acorn cups to hide.

Soon after moonrise on the night before the Duke's wedding, Puck met a fairy in the most beautiful clearing in the whole wood. Puck, a small brown pointy-eared person with slanting blue eyes, was laughing. Already that evening he had stolen a kiss and a bowl of milk from a hard-working housewife and left a silver sixpence in her shoe, and he had pulled the stool out from under a lazy woman and tumbled her on her bottom.

"How now, spirit," he said to the fairy. "Whither wander you?"

"I do wander everywhere, Swifter than the moon's sphere," replied the fairy in a voice like faint chimes. As the deer is much wilder, more delicate and beautiful than the cow, so are fairies much wilder, more delicate and beautiful than mortal men and women. "I serve the Fairy Queen," she said. "I must go seek some dewdrops here, and hang a pearl in every cowslip's ear. Our Queen and all her elves come here anon."

"The King doth keep his revels here tonight. Take heed the Queen come not within his sight, for Oberon is filled with wrath and wild because of that sweet boy, the Indian child." For all his words of warning, Puck spoke cheerfully, and a grin ran right across his freckled face. He served Oberon, but he did not fear him.

"You are that shrewd and knavish sprite called Robin Goodfellow," said the fairy. "Are not you he that frights the maidens of the villagery? Mislead night wanderers, laughing at their harm? Those that call you sweet Puck, you do their work and they shall have good luck. Are you not he?"

And Puck replied, "Thou speaks aright: I am that merry wanderer of the night. I jest to Oberon and make him smile." He laughed and told of how he had teased the church choir and made them laugh so hard they had to quit practice and go home.

Suddenly the moonbeams tingled. The clearing felt alive as never before, as though even the rocks might move of their own accord. Oberon and Titania met in the circle of the trees.

"Ill met by moonlight, proud Titania," said Oberon.

"What, jealous Oberon!" replied Titania, most wild and beautiful of all her people. "Fairies skip hence — I have forsworn his bed and company."

Then the argument began, and the fairies swarmed round Oberon's snakeskin boots, or hid behind the glowing silver Queen. She accused him of stealing away from Fairyland to be with Hippolyta and other mortal women; he accused her of doing the same with Duke Theseus. In truth they were both of them guilty. Titania cried that he broke up her fairy dances, wherever or whenever she might gather her folk, and that the blighted spring was all his doing.

"Why should Titania cross her Oberon?" he asked, softening his voice. "I do but beg a little changeling boy to be my henchman."

"Set your heart at rest," said Titania with a toss of her proud head. "The fairy land can't buy the boy from me." She had promised the dying mother to raise the child in love and honor.

"Ill met by moonlight, proud Titania," said Oberon.

"How long within this wood intend you stay?" demanded Oberon.

"Perchance till after Theseus' wedding day," said Titania.

"Give me that boy and I will go with thee," he bargained.

"No, not for thy fairy kingdom.... Fairies, away!" she retorted, and they disappeared.

Silence filled the glade.

King Oberon stood tall and terrible, brooding, and his crown was sharp as fangs. "Well: go thy way," he said. "Thou shalt not from this grove, till I torment thee for this injury. My gentle Puck, come hither."

Puck stepped forward with his hat in his hand, a floppy dark blue hat like a columbine flower. He made a fancy flourish with it and bowed.

Oberon ordered Puck to find for him a magic flower. "Maidens call it love-in-idleness," he said. "Fetch me that flower. The juice of it, on sleeping eyelids laid, will make man or woman madly love the next living creature that it sees."

"I'll round the earth in forty minutes," cried Puck, and he vanished.

Said Oberon, "I'll watch Titania when she is asleep and drop it in her eyes: the next thing then she looks upon — on lion, or wolf, or meddling monkey — she shall pursue it with the eyes of love."

Voices sounded in the near distance, human voices.

"Who comes here?" said Oberon. "I am invisible, and I will overhear their conference."

Into the silent clearing stumbled Demetrius and Helena. Their fine Athenian clothes were getting dirty struggling through the trees. As they paused for breath, Demetrius said, "I love thee not...therefore pursue me not." He looked about wildly. "Where is Lysander and fair Hermia? Follow me no more."

But Helena could not bear to let him go. "Only give me leave to follow you," she begged.

"I am sick when I do look on you," shouted Demetrius.

"And I am sick when I look not on you," she replied.

"I'll run from thee and hide," he said, "I'll leave thee to the mercy of wild animals."

"The wildest has not such a heart as you," wailed Helena.

Demetrius turned and ran into the wood. Helena gathered up her long skirts and dashed after him.

No branch moved, no bush rustled, but Oberon stood in the clearing once more. "Fare thee well, nymph," he said, gazing after Helena. "Ere he leave this grove, thou shalt fly from him, and he shall seek thy love."

Puck appeared beside him.

"Welcome wanderer," said Oberon. "Hast thou the flower there?"

"Aye," said Puck, "there it is." He was a little out of breath.

"I pray thee, give it me," said Oberon, and he purred with satisfaction. "I know a bank where the wild thyme blows, where oxlips and the nodding violet grows. There sleeps Titania. With the juice of this I'll streak her eyes, and make her full of hateful fantasies."

Then he gave some of the flower juice to Puck and sent him off to find Demetrius and treat his eyes with it so that he would fall in love with Helena. "Thou shalt know the man," instructed Oberon, "by the Athenian garments he has on. Then meet me ere the first cock crow."

Puck took the flower. "Fear not, my lord," he said, "your servant shall do so."

ACT II

Scene 2

TITANIA AND HER FAIRIES lay on a grassy plot beneath the branches of a great oak tree. The air was heavy with the scent of many blossoms.

"Come now, a fairy song," sighed the Fairy Queen. "Sing me now asleep and let me rest."

The fairies began at once to sing a charm to protect their lady as she slept:

> *"You spotted snakes, with double tongue,*
> *Thorny hedgehogs be not seen;*
> *Newts and blind-worms do no wrong,*
> *Come not near our Fairy Queen."*

The beautiful voices of the fairies soon put Titania to sleep. The fairies stole away to a distance to give her privacy while she slept. Even as they waited, surrounding and protecting her, Oberon stepped out of the oak tree beside the sleeping Queen. He waved his hand, and all the fairies joined their Queen in slumber. With two delicate strokes he painted her eyes with the magic flower.

Oberon chanted:

> *"What thou see'st when thou does wake,*
> *Do it for your true love take.*
> *When thou wake it is thy dear:*
> *Wake when some vile thing is near."*

And then he vanished.

With two delicate strokes
he painted her eyes with the magic flower.

The moon climbed a branch or two higher in the sky. Lysander and Hermia approached the grassy plot. The forest by night was a different place, indeed. Wandering lost and tired, they were looking for somewhere to lie down and rest until the coming of the day should reveal their path. Perhaps it was the rays of the moon or perhaps they were so greatly in love with each other that they could see no one else, but neither Lysander nor Hermia saw the Fairy Queen in her enchanted sleep. The grass was most inviting. They laid themselves down, with the tree between them for modesty's sake, as decreed by the customs of Athens.

"Good night, sweet friend," whispered Hermia. "Thy love never alter till thy sweet life end!"

"Amen to that sweet prayer," replied Lysander, "and end my life when I am not true to you!"

So they whispered of their love until they fell asleep.

As they slept, Puck came singing through the wood searching for Demetrius, the Athenian youth whom Oberon had seen treating the lady Helena so badly. When he spied the two lovers sleeping with the tree between them, Puck did not know about modesty and the customs of Athens. He thought the distance was a sign of the man's scorn, and the man must be Demetrius.

"This is he, my master said, despised the Athenian maid," sang Puck to himself, "and here the maiden, sleeping sound, on the dank and dirty ground."

He dripped the flower juice on Lysander's eyes and went away laughing, in search of Oberon.

If no one else had come into the clearing, Lysander would have awakened in the morning and the first person to strike his eye would have been Hermia, and so he would have fallen more in love with her than ever. But this was a night of great confusion in the forest.

The last echoes of Puck's song had all died away. Demetrius burst through the bushes back into the clearing. His clothes were torn and muddy, for the forest clutched and tripped and scratched him as he ran. Helena came close behind, pleading breathlessly for him to stop. But Demetrius tore himself from her grasp and dashed on. He was so busy escaping from her that he never noticed the sleepers in the glade. He just ran off and left Helena, panting and hopeless.

As she stood bemoaning her fate, she spied Lysander. She did not see Hermia beyond the tree. Thinking Lysander wounded or dead, she shook his shoulder; and he, awaking, looked upon her face and fell madly in love with her.

"Not Hermia but Helena I love," he declared. "Who will not change a raven for a dove?"

Helena knew nothing of Puck and the magic flower. She thought Lysander was making fun of her. "When at your hands have I deserved this scorn?" she cried, and she ran off into the woods, weeping.

Lysander took a last look at Hermia sleeping still, but the magic had turned his love for her to hate, and so he ran off after Helena and left his real love lying alone in the forest.

A thin line of cloud cut the moon in half. Hermia slept on, but slowly a nightmare came to her, and she awoke calling to Lysander for help.

"Lysander, look how I do shake with fear," she cried. "Methought a serpent ate my heart away, and you sat smiling at his cruel prey."

She called Lysander's name again and again, but there was no answer. At last she realized that she was left there alone in the forest. She could not think why he would leave her. Fearfully she rose and set off into the trees to find her love. Silence fell again upon the enchanted glade and the sleeping Fairy Queen.

ACT III

Scene 1

THE MOON RODE HIGH AT MIDNIGHT. The cast of *Pyramus and Thisby* straggled into the enchanted glade.

"Here's a marvelous convenient place for our rehearsal," declared Peter Quince. "This green plot shall be our stage, that hawthorn thicket our dressing room, and we will do it in action as we will do it before the Duke." They none of them could see the sleeping silver Fairy Queen, but her magic did steer them to choose their stage across the clearing from her bed of flowers.

"Peter Quince," said Bottom, using his most important voice. "Peter Quince, there are things in this comedy of *Pyramus and Thisby* that will never please. First, Pyramus must draw a sword to kill himself, which the ladies cannot stand. How answer you that?"

"I believe we must leave the killing out," said Starveling, and Tom Snout said the same.

Quince groaned, for the question of how to tell the story of a man who killed himself for love, and yet leave the killing out, made his head hurt. But Bottom had already thought of a better way.

"Write me a prologue," he said, meaning a little speech before the play began, and for once he used the right word. "Let the prologue say we will do no harm with our swords, and that Pyramus is not really killed; that I, Pyramus, am not Pyramus, but Bottom the weaver. This will put them out of fear."

"Will not the ladies be afeared of the lion?" asked Tom Snout.

"A lion among ladies is a most dreadful thing," agreed Bottom. "For there is not a more fearful wildfowl than your lion."

"Therefore," reasoned Snout, slowly, "therefore another prologue must tell he is not a lion."

Peter Quince groaned again, as his play seemed to be stretched longer and longer. Then Nick Bottom saved the day by proclaiming that the first prologue would do, if it named Snug and if part of his face could be seen through his lion mask and if Snug would address the ladies and explain he was just a man in a lion mask.

By the time Bottom was done, Peter Quince found he had promised to recite the whole story of *Pyramus and Thisby* in the prologue. Bottom also recast Tom Snout to play a wall, with a little hole in it that the lovers had whispered their plans through. And fat Robin Starveling was changed to play the moon, by whose light they were to run away.

"Come, sit down," said Peter Quince, trying to get back to business, for it was late, and he wanted to get home to bed. "Sit down, every mother's son, and rehearse your parts. Pyramus," and he nodded at Bottom, "you begin. When you have spoken your speech, enter that thicket and await your cue."

But unknown to Peter Quince, another actor had already entered the scene: Puck, Robin Goodfellow, done with King Oberon's commands and as ready for mischief as a wilderness of monkeys. He looked at the clumsy rough-clad men rehearsing, and his eyes sparkled.

"What hempen homespuns have we swaggering here, so near the cradle of the Fairy Queen? What, a play? I'll be a listener; an actor too, perhaps, if I see cause."

"Speak, Pyramus," said Quince. "Thisby, stand forth."

Pyramus entered —

"If I were handsome, Thisby, I were only thine."

Puck listened to Pyramus begin his first speech, and he thought that Bottom spoke the soft words of love as sweetly as any ass or donkey braying for his lunch. And he thought how someone may be called an ass if he acts stupid or stubborn or self-important. And then he thought how funny it would be if Bottom looked like he sounded, and by that time he was laughing out loud in the shadow of the trees, although nobody heard him. So when the script called for Pyramus to hear a noise and go offstage to see what it was, Puck followed him invisibly into the hawthorn thicket.

"Must I speak now?" asked Flute.

"Ay, must you," said Quince patiently.

"Oh," said Flute. Then he drew a deep breath and raced through every word he was to say in the whole play, all at once, before he lost his nerve.

"Why, you must not speak all that yet," protested Quince, and Snout and Starveling agreed. Snug was trying to practice roaring sweetly, so as not to fright the ladies.

Quince shook his head. They had to keep going, or they'd never get through the play. "Pyramus, enter! Your cue is 'never tire.'"

Flute recalled that line. "Oh," he said, "as true as truest horse, that yet would never tire."

Pyramus entered. "If I were handsome, Thisby," he proclaimed, "I were only thine."

The other actors stood frozen still. Puck had worked his magic in the thicket. Pyramus had Bottom's stocky body, wore his rough clothes, even spoke in Bottom's voice. But the long, grey-haired nose, the dark mane like bangs hanging down between the tall hairy ears: it was not Bottom's head at all, but the head of an ass.

"O, monstrous!" whispered Peter Quince. "O, strange! We are haunted. Pray, masters!" He looked at the others from the corners of his eyes, for he did not like to look away from the monster before him. "Fly, masters!" he cried. "Help!"

They all ran into the woods, and Puck ran to chase them, roaring, mooing, barking, howling. Bottom called after them, but none of them called back, though he could hear them shouting and thrashing through the underbrush for some time.

When at last all was quiet, he scratched his chin. It never occurred to him that his chin was larger and hairier and farther from his chest than usual.

"I see their knavery," said Bottom, one of his long ears twitching. "This is to make an ass of me, to frighten me, if they could. But I will not stir from this place, do what they can. I will walk up and down here, and I will sing, that they shall hear I am not afraid."

And he began to sing at the top of his voice.

"What angel wakes me from my flowery bed?" said Titania, sitting up in the moonlight.

Bottom sang on, though he lost the tune in arguing with himself about what the song said. And then he saw Titania and thought her the most beautiful woman he had ever seen.

"I pray thee, gentle mortal, sing again," said Titania. And as she looked at him, the magic flower did its work on her. "I love thee," she said.

Bottom looked at her doubtfully. No woman had ever said she loved him before, except his mother. "Methinks, mistress, that you have little reason for that. And yet, reason and love keep little company together nowadays."

"What angel wakes me from my flowery bed?"

"Thou art as wise as thou art beautiful," said Titania, now completely under Oberon's spell.

"Not so, neither," said Bottom. She was very beautiful, but he thought it was time for him to go home.

"Out of this wood do not desire to go," she said. "Thou shalt remain here, whether thou wilt or no. I'll give thee fairies to attend on thee, and they shall fetch thee jewels from the deep, and sing while thou on pressed flowers dost sleep. Peaseblossom, Cobweb, Moth, Mustardseed!"

Her fairies all awakened instantly from Oberon's magic sleep. Four of them came running at their Queen's call. Bottom thought them wild and beautiful, but remote and tiny, as if viewed from far away.

"Be kind and courteous to this gentleman," said Titania, softly. "Feed him with apricots and dewberries, with purple grapes, green figs and mulberries; the honey bags steal from humble-bees; pluck the wings from painted butterflies to fan the moonbeams from his sleeping eyes."

"Hail, mortal!" cried Peaseblossom.

"All hail!" cried the others.

Bottom was touched by their courtesy. He asked each their name and made some conversation, doing his best to be polite and use his "company" manners.

In fact, he spoke so long that Titania motioned to the fairies. "Come, wait upon him. Tie up my lover's tongue, bring him silently."

ACT III

Scene 2

OBERON, KING OF THE FAIRIES, returned to the enchanted glade. The moon, golden-brown as old ivory, sank toward the west.

Said Oberon, "I wonder if Titania be awaked; then what it was that next came to her eye. Here comes my messenger. How now, mad spirit?"

Puck trotted out of the forest, a grin on his freckled face as wide and curved as the moon itself. "My mistress with a monster is in love!" he cried, and he burst out laughing. So Puck told Oberon how he had come upon the cast of *Pyramus and Thisby* rehearsing near the Fairy Queen, and how he'd put the ass's head on Bottom, and how at the very sight of Bottom, the others had run shouting away into the woods.

"I led them on in this distracted fear," he said, "and left sweet Pyramus translated there: when in that moment, (so it came to pass) Titania waked and straightway loved an ass!"

Great Oberon shook with mirth. "This falls out better than I could plan. But hast thou yet painted the Athenian's eyes with the love-juice, as I bid thee do?"

"I took him sleeping — that is finished, too," said Puck, quite pleased with himself.

While they spoke, Demetrius and Hermia entered the far side of the clearing.

"Stand close," said Oberon, and he sheltered Puck beneath his magic cloak. "This is the same Athenian."

Puck looked once, then looked again. "This is the woman," he said, "but not this the man."

39

Hermia did not know that the forest had headed her back in a great circle to the same clearing where she and Lysander had whispered of their love before they fell asleep. She stood panting and glaring at Demetrius. She could not understand what had happened to her beloved Lysander. He would never go off and leave her there alone. Something must have happened to him. Searching for him, she had come upon Demetrius. She feared that he had harmed Lysander, but all Demetrius would talk about was how much he loved her.

"Where is he?" she pleaded. "Ah, good Demetrius, wilt thou give him to me?"

"I had rather give his carcass to my hounds," said Demetrius.

"Hast thou slain him then?" she cried.

He shook his head. "I am not guilty of Lysander's blood, he is not dead for all that I can tell."

"I pray thee," said Hermia, "tell me then that he is well."

Said Demetrius, "And if I could, what should I get therefore?"

And Hermia replied, "The privilege never to see me anymore!" And she ran away into the wood.

Demetrius sighed. "There is no use following her in this fierce vein," he said to himself, sadly. He was so tired that he sat down to rest, and before many minutes had passed he had begun to snore.

Oberon flung his cape behind him. His eyes blazed with wrath. Puck skipped up a tree and sat on a limb just out of reach.

"What hast thou done?" demanded Oberon. "Thou hast mistaken quite and laid the love-juice on some true-love's sight. Some true-love now is turned false, not a false turned true."

Puck laughed and tried to make a joke, but Oberon would have none of it. "About the wood, go swifter than the wind," he commanded, "and Helena of Athens look thou find. By some illusion see thou bring her here: I'll charm his eyes and then she will appear."

Puck leaped down from the tree. "I go, I go — look how I go — swifter than an arrow from a Tartar's bow." And he vanished.

Oberon bent over the sleeping Demetrius. "Flower of this purple dye," he whispered, "sink in the apple of his eye when his love he does espy."

Puck reappeared and saluted with his big blue hat. "Captain of our fairy band, Helena is here at hand, and the youth mistook by me." He laughed, for he was pleased with his prank. Two men who loved Hermia would be translated into two men who loved Helena. He laughed again. "Lord, what fools these mortals be!"

Helena did not recognize the clearing. She was tired, and bits of sticks and leaves were tangled in her long blond hair. She did not know that she stood once again in the clearing where first she found Lysander sleeping on the ground.

Helena wished with all her heart that she had never waked him up. She had fled blindly from him, while he followed pleading of his love for her. How could Lysander say such things to her, when all the world knew he loved her best friend, Hermia? Helena was sure he must be making fun of her. He didn't love her any more than did Demetrius. He must be making fun.

As she stood trembling, uncertain which way to turn, Demetrius awoke. He sat up and looked around, and he saw tall, blond Helena by moonlight, and Oberon's magic did its work.

"O Helena," he said, his blue eyes burning with devotion, "O goddess, nymph, perfect, divine!"

Helena was struck dumb. It was what she'd always dreamed Demetrius would say, but now that it had come, how could she believe him? That very night he'd said it made him sick to look at her; he'd run away to leave her at the mercy of wild beasts. He must be making fun of her, too. He and Lysander both were making fun of her.

Then came the most confusing part of the whole night in the forest. Demetrius and Lysander fell to arguing, just as they had done in the Duke's hall; only now each claimed to love Helena, not Hermia. Meanwhile poor Hermia, wandering lost, heard their loud voices and followed the sound to the clearing. She ran at once to her beloved Lysander, but he pushed her away, and he proclaimed his new love for Helena. But Helena, watching them, was convinced that all their talk was made-up to hurt her, and that Hermia had joined the men to mock her.

When Lysander said, "Helena, I love thee — by my life I do," Demetrius shouted back, "I say I love thee more than he can do."

Lysander faced Demetrius and drew his sword. "If thou say so," he said, "draw, and prove it too."

Then did Hermia believe that Lysander loved Helena, and the confusion was complete. "Thief of love," she cried to Helena. "Have you come by night and stolen Lysander's heart from him?"

But Helena still thought Hermia was making fun of her. "You counterfeit," she answered. "You puppet."

Knowing they should not shed blood in sight of the ladies,
the men marched grimly off into the woods to fight a duel.

Petite Hermia was most sensitive about being short. "Puppet?" she screamed at tall Helena. "I am not yet so small but that my nails may reach your eyes!"

Helena shrunk back. "Let her not strike me!" she pleaded. "Though she be but little, she is fierce."

Now there were two fights going on. Hermia struggled to grab Helena by the hair, while Demetrius and Lysander threatened each other with their swords. Knowing they should not shed blood in sight of the ladies, the men marched grimly off into the woods to fight a duel.

Hermia looked at Helena. "Mistress," she said, threateningly, "this trouble is because of you."

Helena backed away, then turned and fled into the trees. Hermia ran after her, shrieking threats at the top of her voice.

Oberon turned to Puck with a look like lightning across the night sky. "This is thy negligence. Still thou mistak'st, or else commit thy knaveries willfully."

"Believe me, king of shadows, I mistook," cried Puck. "I have anointed an Athenian's eyes. And so far am I glad it so did sort, for this their jangling I esteem a sport."

Oberon silenced him with a glance. "These lovers seek a place to fight. Hie therefore, Robin, overcast the night, and lead these testy rivals so astray as one comes not within another's way. Lead them thus till over their brows, sleep doth creep. Then crush this herb into Lysander's eyes to take all error from his sight." Oberon sighed. "When next they wake, all this shall seem a dream and fruitless vision.

Meanwhile, go I to my queen and beg the disputed Indian boy. Then I will her charmed eye release from monster's view, and all things shall be peace."

"My fairy lord," said Puck, "this must be done in haste."

"Make no delay," commanded Oberon. "We may effect our business yet ere day." And he disappeared.

Puck whirled with his arms spread wide, spinning and spinning, and he chanted:

"Up and down, up and down,
I will lead them up and down.
I am feared in field and town.
Goblin lead them up and down!"

Thick black fog came up from the ground, shutting out the moon. The night grew dark as ink beneath the trees.

Out in the wood, Lysander could not see his hand before his face. "Where art thou, proud Demetrius?" he called.

"Here, villain!" replied Puck.

Lysander leaped toward the voice, but he tripped over a root and fell into a prickly bush.

Elsewhere, Demetrius stumbled through the inky dark. "Lysander! Speak again!" he called.

"Coward, bragging to the stars," jeered Puck, in Lysander's voice.

Demetrius ran toward the voice, but a tree branch caught him in the ribs and sent him sprawling.

Puck teased and tormented them, leading them in circles, while the forest beat from them all of their fury and their strength. In the end, he led them back to the enchanted glade, and first one, then the other, laid them down to sleep there.

And Puck did the same with Helena and Hermia. He called each with the other's voice, and chased them with howl of wolf and roar of lion until both staggered in their weariness. Their dresses were torn by the briars and thorns and stained with moss and mud. Sticks and bits of bark were stuck in Hermia's dark curly hair. At the very last he drew them, too, back to the enchanted glade.

First came Helena, who wanted nothing more than for the night to end, so she could go home. In the dark how could she know that Puck had steered her to lie down to sleep but arm's length from Demetrius?

Puck laughed. "Yet but three?" he said. "Come one more. Two of both kinds makes up four. Here she comes, cursed and sad. Cupid is a knavish lad, thus to make poor females mad."

Then came Hermia, her eyelids so heavy, her heart so sad, so confused. The last words she said before sleep were to pray for her beloved Lysander. And she laid herself down to sleep, not knowing he lay so close, she could have reached out and touched him.

Puck rolled the sleeping Lysander over so that he would wake face to face with Hermia, his true love, then dripped the love-juice on Lysander's eyelids.

"When thou wake," chanted Puck, "thou take true delight in the sight of thy former lady's eye." He looked around at his handiwork, satisfied that now everything would work out right. "Jack shall have Jill; and all shall be well," he said. And he vanished.

The fog cleared away. The old moon seemed to stretch out across half the sky in a final yawn before it rolled off to bed.

A C T   I V

Scene 1

THE STARS GREW PALE IN THE SKY. The birds had not yet begun to sing to the dawn; they kept to their nests but murmured in their sleep. In the enchanted glade, the four lovers slumbered on, little dreaming that true love would find them with the sun.

Into the clearing came Bottom and Titania, followed by her fairies. They had danced all the night since the Queen found her new love. Bottom wore chains of flowers round his hairy neck and tucked behind his long, twitching ears. He looked more apt to eat the flowers than to wear them.

"Come sit thee down upon this flowery bed," Titania said to Bottom, "while I do stick roses in thy smooth sleek hair, and kiss thy fair large ears, my gentle joy."

Bottom sat down beside her. He had enjoyed the fairy dancing, but he was tired and hungry and ready for rest. He did admit it was very pleasant to have Titania's sweet smooth arms around him and all her fairies at his beck and call. Cobweb brought him honeycombs, while Peaseblossom and Mustardseed scratched his chin and behind his ears.

"I must to the barber's," said Bottom, "for methinks I am marvelously hairy about the face — and I am such a tender ass, if my hair do but tickle me, I must scratch."

"Wilt thou hear some music, my sweet love?" asked Titania. "Or say what thou desire to eat."

"I pray you, let none stir me," said Bottom with a grand yawn. "I have an exposition of sleep come upon me."

47

"Come sit thee down upon this flowery bed
while I do stick roses in thy smooth sleek hair,
and kiss thy fair large ears, my gentle joy."

"Sleep thou," said Titania, "and I will wrap thee in my arms. Fairies be gone," she said, and then, "O, how I love thee," and they both fell asleep.

Then came Oberon and Puck, who looked upon Titania and her ass-headed lover.

"Welcome good Robin," said Oberon to Puck. "See'st thou this sweet sight?" Their laughter was almost enough to awaken the birds. He pointed at the flowers in Bottom's hair. "See how the dew stands now within the pretty flowerets' eyes like tears that do their own disgrace bewail."

Oberon raised his fist in triumph. "Just now, within the wood, I have asked Titania for the disputed Indian boy, which straight she gave me. Her fairy is sent to bring him to Fairyland." Oberon laughed. He had won his argument with Titania. Her love for Bottom had melted her willfulness. Now together the King and Queen would raise the boy in love and honor. "And now I have the boy," he said, "I will undo this hateful imperfection of her eyes. And Puck, take off this ass's head from this Athenian, that he, waking, may to Athens back again, and think no more of this night's accidents but as the fierce vexation of a dream."

Puck bowed low.

"But first," said Oberon, "I must release the Fairy Queen."

Oberon painted Titania's eyes with the magic flower. "Be as thou was wont to be; see as thou was wont to see. Now, my Titania! Wake you, my sweet Queen."

Titania opened her eyes. "My Oberon!" she said. "What visions have I seen! Methought I was in love with an ass."

"There lies your love," said Oberon, pointing.

Titania shrank back from the snoring Bottom. "How came these things to pass? O, how mine eyes do loathe him now."

"Robin, take off this head," said Oberon. "Titania, music call, to strike deeper than common sleep upon these five." And he gestured to Bottom and the sleeping lovers.

"Music, ho!" called Titania. "Music such as charmeth sleep." And her fairies began to play magic music.

Puck broke his spell and whipped the ass's head off Bottom, who just rolled over and snored all the louder.

"Come, my queen, take hands with me," said Oberon. As they began to dance, he said to her, "Tomorrow midnight solemnly we dance in Duke Theseus' house triumphantly, and bless it to all fair prosperity. There shall the pairs of faithful lovers be wedded, with Theseus, all in jollity."

"Come, my lord," said Titania, looking at Oberon with loving eyes, "and in our flight, tell me how it came this night that I sleeping here was found with these mortals on the ground."

And they flew away with the vanishing night, faint notes of their music trailing after.

There was a great bustle now among the birds. When the first rays of sunlight streamed over the hill and combed the tangled forest with slender golden fingers, the birds all burst into song.

Then came the sound of hunting horns, borne down the faint breeze of dawn. Duke Theseus and his bride, Queen Hippolyta, and all their court were out early with their hounds. The Duke and his bride loved to follow their hounds over hill and vale, through forest and fen. It was a beautiful morning for their wedding day. The long baying cries of the hounds echoed through the forest in musical confusion.

As Theseus and Hippolyta followed on, they entered into a clearing in the wood and beheld the lovers sleeping on the ground.

"What nymphs are these?" asked Theseus, smiling down at the sleepers.

Hermia's father, old Egeus, pushed forward through the lords and ladies. "My lord, this is my daughter here asleep. And this, Lysander, Demetrius, Helena. I wonder of their being here together."

"Speak, Egeus," said the Duke. "Was this not the day that Hermia should give answer of her choice?"

"It is, my lord," said Egeus.

The Duke nodded. "Go, bid the huntsmen wake them with their horns."

The horns blew loudly; the four lovers leaped up, all startled, with their eyes still full of sleep.

"Good morrow, friends," said Theseus.

"Pardon, my lord," said Lysander, and the rest chorused, "Pardon," after him as they knelt.

"I pray you all, stand up," said the Duke. He looked at them curiously. "I know you two are rivals," he said to Lysander and Demetrius. "How comes it that hatred sleeps by hate and fears not?"

But Lysander could not say how he came to be there, nor could any of the others. He could remember stealing forth from Athens with Hermia, to escape her father and the cruel law. Old Egeus sputtered, but the Duke called for silence. Hermia ran to Lysander's side, and he looked with his old love into her eyes.

Demetrius could remember chasing after them, but somehow during the night his love for Hermia had melted away, until he could barely remember it. It was Helena he loved, and he would forever more. He gave up willingly all claim to Hermia, here before the Duke. He clasped hands with Helena, who looked at him with all her joy. Then the two couples turned to Theseus to hear what justice he would declare.

Egeus opened his mouth, but Theseus raised his hand. "Egeus," he said, "I will overbear your will. For in the temple, this day, with us, these couples shall be eternally wed. Away with us to Athens! Three and three, we'll hold a feast in great solemnity. Come, Hippolyta," he said, and held out his arm to her.

The four lovers stayed a moment longer in the clearing after the court moved away. Each one was struggling with memories of that midsummer's night.

"Are you sure that we are well awake?" asked Demetrius. "It seems to me that yet we sleep, we dream. Do you not think the Duke was here and bid us follow him?"

"Yes," said Hermia, "and my father."

"And Hippolyta and all the court," added Helena.

"And he did bid us follow him to the temple," said Lysander.

"Why then, we are awake," said Demetrius, thankfully.

And off they went, arm in arm, talking and laughing all together. Above them, larks sang love songs in the sky. Beside them, the tiny wildflowers bathed their paths in faint perfume. And in the enchanted glade, the sun poured buttery across the glowing green grass.

A warm golden sunbeam pierced the forest leaves and shone on sleeping Bottom's face and tickled his nose until he sneezed. Sitting up, he yawned and rubbed his eyes.

"When my cue comes, call me, and I will answer," he said sleepily, for he thought he was still rehearsing the play with his friends. "Heigh-ho!" He yawned again and looked about him. "Peter Quince! Flute! Snout! Starveling! What? Stolen hence, and left me asleep!

"I have had a most rare vision," he said to himself. "I have had a dream — past the wit of man to say what dream it was. Man is but an ass if he go about to explain this dream." Bottom shook his head. "The eye of man hath not heard, the ear of man hath not seen, man's hand is not able to taste, his tongue to conceive, nor his heart to report what my dream was."

Then another thought came to him. "I will get Peter Quince to write a ballad of this dream," he said. "It shall be called Bottom's Dream, because it hath no bottom. And I will sing it as an epilogue, at the end of our play, before the Duke."

And whistling cheerfully, Bottom set off for home.

ACT IV

Scene 2

IN THE CITY OF ATHENS, the cast of *Pyramus and Thisby* met in Peter Quince's cottage.

Have you sent to Bottom's house?" demanded Peter Quince. "Is he come home yet?"

"He cannot be heard of," said Starveling, and Tom Snout nodded sad agreement.

"If he come not, then the play is marred," mourned Flute. "It goes not forward, doth it?"

"It is not possible," said Quince, shaking his head. "You have not a man in all Athens able to play Pyramus but he."

Snug the joiner hurried in. "Masters, the Duke is coming from the temple, and there is two or three lords and ladies more married. If our sport had gone forward, we had all been made men."

The others nodded, for performing before such a splendid audience would surely have brought each man a royal reward, and Bottom, the hero, most of all.

Their faces were as long as sad horses, when suddenly the door burst open, and there stood Bottom, his old self again.

"Where are these lads?" he cried. "Where are these hearts?"

"Bottom! O most happy hour!" shouted Quince, and with a cry of welcome, the others threw themselves upon Bottom, hugging and punching him and slapping his back, demanding to know all his adventures.

Suddenly the door burst open,
and there stood Bottom, his old self again.
"Where are these lads? Where are these hearts?"

"Masters, I could discourse wonders," said Bottom, grandly.

"Let us hear, sweet Bottom," begged Peter Quince, and the others stood, mouths agape, to hear these wonders told.

"Not a word of me," replied Bottom, and their faces fell again. "All that I will tell you is — that the Duke hath dined. Get all your costumes together; meet presently at the palace; every man look over his part; for the long and short of it is, our play is chosen!"

The others all cheered. Bottom raised his arms for quiet. "Let Thisby have clean linen, and he that plays the lion (Snug looked up anxiously), let him not cut his nails, for they shall hang out for the lion's claws. And, most dear actors, eat no onions or garlic, for we are to utter most sweet breath. Away!"

ACT V

Scene 1

S O THE LOVERS WERE MARRIED that very day in the great temple of Athens, along with the Duke and his bride. The city went mad with joy. Music filled the air. The wedding party's path from the temple back to the palace was strewn with flowers. A great banquet then was held, so grand the cooks used peacocks for table decorations.

After dinner, Hippolyta and Theseus went into the great hall for entertainment.

"'Tis strange, my Theseus," she said, "what these lovers speak of."

"More strange than true," he answered. "I never can believe these antic fables, nor these fairy toys. Lovers and madmen have such seething brains."

"But all the story of the night told over, and all their minds transfigured so together," she protested.

"Here come the lovers, full of joy and mirth," said Theseus. "Come now, what masques, what dances shall we have to while away this long age of three hours between our after-supper and bed-time? Call Philostrate."

Then came Philostrate, the master of the Duke's revels. "Here, mighty Theseus," he said, and bowed, and gave to him a list of plays and musical groups and speeches they might listen to.

Theseus read down the list, but nothing pleased his fancy. Then he stopped and read aloud, "'A tedious brief scene of young Pyramus and his love Thisby; very tragical mirth.' Merry and tragical?" he said, and smiled. "Tedious and brief? That is hot ice and wondrous strange snow."

"There is a play," explained Philostrate, "some ten words long, which is as brief as I have known a play; but by ten words, my lord, it is too long, which makes it tedious. And tragical, my lord, for Pyramus doth kill himself, yet when I saw it rehearsed, I must confess, more merry tears loud laughter never shed."

"Then we will hear it," said the Duke, and the cast of *Pyramus and Thisby* was called for. All the lords and ladies of the court took seats behind their Duke to watch the entertainment.

The whole cast came forth to bow to their audience. First came Bottom as Pyramus, with a wooden sword in a scabbard belted round his broad waist. Then came Francis Flute as the lady Thisby, with his wig on crooked and black makeup painted heavily around his eyes. Next was Tom Snout, who played the Wall, with plaster smeared on his shirt and a brick in his hand, and last came Robin Starveling, with his lantern, dog and bundle of thorns, to portray Moonshine.

Peter Quince nervously stammered out his prologue, the whole story: how the lovers ran away to meet at Ninus' Tomb, how the lion roared to frighten Thisby who dropped her scarf, how lion got blood from his last meal on her scarf, which being found by Pyramus, made him think that Thisby was dead, and how he killed himself for sadness at the loss of her, and she coming after and finding him dead, killed herself likewise. The words rattled out like marbles on a tile floor, and the moment he finished, Peter Quince ducked into safety behind the curtain.

"I wonder if the lion be to speak," said Theseus.

"No wonder, my lord," said Demetrius. "One lion may, when so many asses do."

The stage was now cleared, and from behind the curtain came Wall, smeared with plaster, brick in hand, who bowed and said, "I, one Snout by name, present a wall that had in it a hole or chink," and he stretched forth his fingers to make that chink, "through which the lovers, Pyramus and Thisby, did whisper very often secretly." He stood in the center of the stage with his arms spread wide.

Then came Pyramus, peering here and there, his hand upon his sword hilt to leave no doubt he came in secrecy and danger of his life. "O grim-looked night!" he proclaimed loudly. "O night with hue so black! O night which ever art when day is not! O night, O night, alack, alack, alack. O wall, that stands between her father's land and mine, show me thy chink to blink through with mine eyne." He tried to peer through Wall's fingers, but Snout was very tall, and his hand was over Bottom's head, so as the audience chuckled, lover Pyramus had to jump and catch the arm and pull it down.

"Thanks, courteous wall," said Pyramus, glaring at him. "But what see I? No Thisby do I see. Cursed be thy stones for thus deceiving me!" He whacked Wall on the shoulder. Snout staggered, then stiffened into Wall again.

Flute, dressed as Thisby, entered, stepped hard upon unaccustomed skirts and fell flat on his face. The audience laughed. Thisby scrambled to her feet, straightened her wig and cried, "O wall! Full often hast thou heard my moans, for parting my fair Pyramus and me."

"I see a voice," said Pyramus, ducking the brick in Wall's outstretched hand. "Now will I to the chink, to spy if I can hear my Thisby's face. Thisby!"

"My love!" cried Thisby, ducking in turn as Wall swung back. "Thou art my love, I think." Flute was not certain if that was the right line to say.

"O! Kiss me through the hole of this vile wall," said Pyramus.

They pressed their lips on either side of Snout's fingers and made loud kissing sounds. Snout drew back his hand and wiped it on his pants.

"I kiss the wall's hole, not your lips at all," complained Thisby.

"Wilt thou at Ninny's Tomb meet me straightaway?" asked Pyramus.

Thisby knew the response to that. "Come life, come death," she said, "I come without delay."

Pyramus strode behind the curtain. Flute, done with his lines and afraid of being left alone on the stage, ran after him, almost toppling the wall that supposedly divided Thisby from her love.

Snout faced the audience. "Thus have I, Wall, my part discharged so; and being done, thus Wall away doth go." And he slipped behind the curtain with a loud sigh of relief.

"This is the silliest stuff that ever I heard," said Hippolyta.

Theseus smiled graciously. "The best of actors are but shadows," he replied, "and the worst are no worse, if imagination amend them."

"It must be your imagination then; and not theirs," she replied.

Snug the joiner shuffled out from behind the curtain. His lion mask was pushed back on his head to reveal his apprehensive face, for he had come to keep the ladies from being frightened. "You ladies, you whose gentle hearts do fear the smallest monstrous mouse that creeps on floor," he said, "may now perchance both quake and tremble here, when lion rough in wildest rage doth roar. Then know that I, as Snug the joiner, am the lion fierce, and let not fears your ladies hearts do pierce."

"A very gentle beast," said Theseus, "and of a good conscience."

"The very best at a beast that ever I saw," laughed Demetrius.

Fat Robin Starveling now came out. "This lantern," said he, "doth the horned moon present; myself the man in the moon do seem to be."

"This is the greatest error of all the rest," laughed Theseus. "The man should be put into the lantern. How else is it the man in the moon?"

"He dares not come there for the candle," said Demetrius.

"I am aweary of this moon," sighed Hippolyta. "Would he would change!"

"Proceed, Moon," called Lysander.

Starveling was determined not to be interrupted again. With a deep breath, he raced through all his lines at once. "All I have to say is to tell you that the lantern is the moon, I, the man in the moon, this thornbush is my thornbush, and this dog, my dog." And he held his lantern high.

Thisby peeked out from behind the curtain, uncertain if her cue had come. Peter Quince sent her out onstage with a hearty shove. Her eye make-up was so smeared she seemed to be wearing a black mask.

"This is old Ninny's Tomb," said Thisby, straightening her wig again and looking around. "Where is my love?"

Lion roared, a delicate and gentlemanly roar. You could almost see him cover his mouth, as if it were a cough. Thisby shrieked and ran behind the curtain. A moment later, her scarf flew back onstage and landed in a heap, thrown by Peter Quince since Flute had forgotten to drop it. The audience doubled over with laughter.

"Well roared, Lion," said Demetrius.

"Well run, Thisby," said the Duke.

"Well shone, Moon," said Hippolyta.

Snug the Lion picked up Thisby's scarf and tried to tear it to pieces with his teeth, so Pyramus would find it bloody from the Lion's mouth. The scarf was too tough though, so he wiped his face with it and threw it down.

"Well moused, Lion," said Theseus.

So anxious was Snug to escape the stage that he almost ran over Pyramus, who was trying to enter.

"And so the lion vanished," chuckled Lysander.

Pyramus proclaimed, "Sweet moon, I thank thee for thy sunny beams."

The audience dissolved in laughter once again. Pyramus picked up the soggy scarf and held it at arm's length. "Eyes, do you see? How can it be? Thy mantle good, what, stained with blood?" Pyramus wailed the loss of his love, for he believed the lion had eaten her.

Said Theseus, wiping his eyes, "This play—and the death of a dear friend—would go near to make a man look sad."

Bottom pulled the wooden sword out of the scabbard and waved it in the air before plunging it between his arm and chest and clamping it there. "Now am I dead," he proclaimed. "Now am I fled, my soul is in the sky. Tongue lose thy light! Moon, take thy flight! (Starveling did

"Now am I dead," he proclaimed.

"Now am I fled, my soul is in the sky."

not remember that as being in the script, but he obligingly galloped offstage.) Now, die, die, die, die, die." And Bottom spun around three times, groaned, and fell to the stage with a heavy thud. The sword cracked loudly as it broke beneath him.

The audience was in tears, but they were not tears of sorrow. They had never seen anything so funny in their lives.

"No die, but an ace for him," said Demetrius.

"With the help of a surgeon, he might yet recover," said the Duke, as they watched Pyramus, panting heavily, lying dead on the stage.

"How chance Moonshine is gone before Thisby comes back and finds her lover?" asked Hippolyta.

"She will find him by starlight," replied Theseus. "Here she comes, and her grieving ends the play."

"Methinks she should not be long at it for such a Pyramus," said Hippolyta.

"She hath spied him already with those sweet eyes," said Lysander.

Flute had tried to fix his makeup, but he would forget and rub his face. With his hands blackened and smeary cheeks, and the handprints on his skirt, his Thisby looked as though she had been cleaning chimneys on her way to Ninus' Tomb. When he came out on stage everyone laughed so hard that Flute forgot his line and stared at them. He didn't watch where he was going, and so he fell over Bottom.

Desperate to complete the scene, Flute tried to recall the right words. "Asleep my love? What, dead my dove?" he shrilled, scrambling to his knees and pulling his skirt down. "These lily lips, this cherry nose, these yellow cowslip cheeks," said Thisby, poking Pyramus in the eye while reaching for her handkerchief. "Gone, all gone. Lovers make moan. His eyes were green as leeks." Thisby reached for Pyramus' sword to kill herself, but it was not in sight. Her next line was, "Come, trusty sword," and then she was to stab herself, just as Pyramus had done, but where was the sword?

"Come, trusty sword," said Flute, almost in tears, for he saw no way to escape this endless play unless he could kill himself. "Come, trusty sword," he said again, desperately. He found the handle of the sword, but the blade was broken off just below the hilt. The blade was under Bottom, and Bottom was too heavy for him to move. "Come, trusty sword," he said for the third time, searching for anything even remotely sword-shaped that he could use, when at last his eye lit upon the scabbard to Pyramus' sword. The belt had come loose in Pyramus' great death flounderings. Flute seized it.

"Come, trusty sword," he cried, whacking himself with the blunt end of it and falling heavily across Bottom's chest. He lay panting for a moment, while the audience wiped their eyes and held their sides. Then he raised his head. "Farewell friends," he said. "Thus Thisby ends. Adieu, adieu, adieu."

Moonshine, Lion and Wall slowly drew the curtains together on the dead lovers.

When the applause and laughter had died away, Duke Theseus said, "Moonshine and Lion are left to bury the dead."

"Ay, and Wall, too," said Demetrius.

"No, I assure you," said Snug the Lion earnestly. "The wall is down that parted their fathers. Will it please you to see the epilogue, or to hear a dance?"

"No epilogue, I pray you," said Theseus, "for your play needs no excuse. Never excuse, for when the players are all dead, there is none left to be blamed. Come, your dance."

At that, Pyramus and Thisby picked themselves up and joined Lion and Wall in a spirited dance, while Quince and Starveling played the pipe and drum.

When the dance was done, Theseus rose. In the distance, a clock chimed as he spoke. "The iron tongue of midnight hath told twelve!" he said. "Lovers, to bed — 'tis almost fairy time. I fear we shall outsleep the coming morn."

Then Bottom and his friends returned most joyfully to Peter Quince's cottage, there to celebrate their good fortune and tell and retell the tale until the dawn. Duke Theseus and his court climbed the long sweeping stairways to their bed chambers. And in the great hall all was still.

It was the dark of the moon, the new moon, that shows not the slightest sliver of light in the sky. The palace lay cleaned and swept for the next day's celebration, for the wedding festivities were to last two weeks. Tired housemaids swept the last dust behind doors, hoping to escape a scolding, and trudged off to bed.

A little gust of wind stirred and danced and tickled through the palace, sweeping out all the hidden dustballs, scurrying them across the floor and into the dying fire in the great fireplace, where they flamed into nothingness and disappeared.

Then came Puck, Robin Goodfellow, sitting in the Duke's chair, holding a broom the way the Duke held his scepter, and he laughed at the Duke and the lovers as they had laughed at the play. He chanted:

> *"Now the hungry lion roars*
> *And the wolf behowls the moon;*
> *Whilst the heavy plowman snores,*
> *All with weary task fordone.*
> *And we fairies, that do run from the presence of the sun,*
> *Following darkness like a dream, now may frolic.*
> *Not a mouse shall disturb this hallowed house…*
> *I am sent with broom before,*
> *To sweep the dust behind the door."*

Then, in a blaze of pearl-grey fire came Oberon and Titania, King and Queen of the Fairies, and all their people.

Only Puck was left, leaning on his broom.

And he said: "Give me your hands, if we be friends..."

King Oberon spoke: "Now until the break of day, through this house each fairy stray. And each several chamber bless, through this palace with sweet peace. And the owner of it, blessed, ever shall in safety rest. So shall all the couples three ever true in loving be. Trip away; make no stay; meet me all by break of day."

All night the fairies passed from room to room, blessing the Duke and all his people, until just before the first rooster opened his eyes the next morning. Then Oberon called them all together, and they rode away on the wings of his power, chasing the night.

Only Puck was left, leaning on his broom. And he said:

> *"If we shadows have offended,*
> *Think but this, and all is mended,*
> *That you have but slumbered here*
> *While these visions did appear.*
> *And this weak and idle theme,*
> *No more yielding but a dream.*
> *Gentles, do not reprehend.*
> *If you pardon, we will mend.*
> *Give me your hands, if we be friends,*
> *And Robin shall restore amends.*

EPILOGUE

Now that you know the story, perhaps you'd like to play out a bit of *A Midsummer Night's Dream* for yourself. An actor studies a script to learn all of the words and movements that the part requires. You'll find playscripts in the envelope inside the back cover of the book. If you take them out, you will see two short scenes between Titania, Queen of the Fairies, and Nick Bottom, when Puck had put the ass's head on him.

The first thing is to decide what part you want to play. Each scene is really for two people, one to play Bottom and one to play Titania, though there are small parts for the Fairies. If you only have two people for the scene, the person playing Titania can also do the voices of the fairies when they talk with Bottom.

Read your parts over so you make sure you can say all the words. If you want to, you can memorize the words by saying them over and over until you know them by heart. That's how the actors do it. Let the words roll off your tongue for the sound of them, even if you don't understand them all at first. Remember, half the fun in these scenes comes because Bottom never understands that Puck has made him wear an ass's head. The other half comes because Titania can see the ass's head, but believes it is the most beautiful thing she has ever seen.

Some sentences on the script cards are written in italics. Those are the stage directions. They tell the actors where the scene is taking place, when people go on and off stage, and if they stand up or sit down, sing or go to sleep.

You can have fun making costumes or you can just pretend. The important thing is to use your imagination. For Titania, any kind of cape, even a piece of gauze, will do. You can make a crown from cardboard and aluminum foil or woven sticks painted silver. Make paper flowers to hang about Bottom's neck. For Bottom, you could make just a pair of cardboard ears, or put them on an old baseball cap and spray it gray, with string down the back for a mane and white paper eyes glued just above the bill. Make a paper bag mask. Turn your imagination loose.

You can make your stage indoors or out. Indoors, use a doorway or an arch to hang a curtain to play the play in front of, and exit behind. Outdoors, play the scenes in a yard or garden or park; use a bush or a hedge to hide you when you go off stage. Find a porch, or the landing of a stairway. Make sure there's room for your audience to sit and watch the play.

Hold this picture in your mind. Everyone gets quiet, and your play begins, and magic happens. All at once you are Titania and foolish Nick Bottom, meeting at midnight in the Palace Wood, under an enchanted moon. You and the audience will make magic together.

Pronunciation Guide

THESEUS .... THĒ'-sē-ŭs

HIPPOLYTA .... Hĭ-PĂL'-ĭ-tă

EGEUS .... Ē'-jŭs

LYSANDER .... Lī-SĂN'-dŭr

DEMETRIUS .... Dĭ-MĒT'-rē-ŭs

HERMIA .... HĔR'-mē-ă

HELENA .... HĔL'-ĭ-nă

OBERON .... Ō'-bŭ-rŏn

TITANIA .... Tī-TĀ'-nē-ă

ā = ape, ă = ah, ē = even, ĕ = end, ī = ice, ĭ = hip, ō = open, ŏ = on, ŭ = us

PETER V.T. KAHLE has directed two nonprofessional productions of Shakespeare's *A Midsummer Night's Dream*. He has been a teacher, a stained glass artist, and a lacrosse referee. He is a past president of the Pacific Northwest Writers Conference, a member of the Literary Arts Alliance and a founder of the Collective Wheee. This is his first book for young people. He lives in Seattle, Washington, with his wife.

BARBARA NICKERSON'S enchanting watercolor illustrations grew out of a long fascination with Shakespeare. She has shown her work in New York, Germany, and had a solo exhibition in Paris. She is listed in both the *Encyclopedia of Sumi-E* and *Who's Who in International Sumi-E Artists*. She received her BFA at the Art Institute of Chicago, and is a workshop teacher and signature member of the Northwest Watercolor Society, Women Painters of Washington and Puget Sound Sumi Artists. Barbara lives on a ranch in Cle Elum, Washington, with her husband.